Anxiety Journal

INFORMATIONS

NAME

ADDRESS

E-MAIL ADDRESS

WEBSITE

PHONE   **FAX**

EMERGENCY CONTACT PERSON

PHONE   **FAX**

© 2021 MILLIE ZOES

All rights reserved.
No part of this publication may be reproduced, distributed or transmitted in any form or by any means including photocopying, recording or other electronic or mechanical methods without the prior written permission of the publisher, except in the case of brief quotations embodied in critical reviews and certain other non commercial uses permitted by copyright law.

Thank you for your recent purchase.

If you wouldn't mind leaving an online review section, we would really appreciate that. We love hearing everyone thoughts and comments.

Anxiety Journal

DATE   TIME

PLACE   SOURCE OF ANXIETY

PHYSICAL SENSATIONS

NEGATIVE BELIEVES

ABOUT SITUATION ....
....

ABOUT YOUSELF ....
....

WHAT FACTS DO YOU KNOW ARE TRUE?

ABOUT SITUATION ....
....

ABOUT YOUSELF ....
....

WHAT HAPPENED?

....
....

HOW DID IT MAKE YOU FEEL?

....
....

HOW DID YOU REACT?

....
....

WHAT HELPS YOU SOOTHE YOUR ANXIETY?

....
....

Anxiety Journal

DATE   **TIME**

PLACE   **SOURCE OF ANXIETY**

PHYSICAL SENSATIONS

NEGATIVE BELIEVES

ABOUT SITUATION ....
....

ABOUT YOUSELF ....
....

WHAT FACTS DO YOU KNOW ARE TRUE?

ABOUT SITUATION ....
....

ABOUT YOUSELF ....
....

WHAT HAPPENED?

....
....

HOW DID IT MAKE YOU FEEL?

....
....

HOW DID YOU REACT?

....
....

WHAT HELPS YOU SOOTHE YOUR ANXIETY?

....
....

Anxiety Journal

DATE   TIME

PLACE   SOURCE OF ANXIETY

PHYSICAL SENSATIONS

NEGATIVE BELIEVES

ABOUT SITUATION ....
....

ABOUT YOUSELF ....
....

WHAT FACTS DO YOU KNOW ARE TRUE?

ABOUT SITUATION ....
....

ABOUT YOUSELF ....
....

WHAT HAPPENED?

....
....

HOW DID IT MAKE YOU FEEL?

....
....

HOW DID YOU REACT?

....
....

WHAT HELPS YOU SOOTHE YOUR ANXIETY?

....
....

Anxiety Journal

DATE .... **TIME** ....

PLACE .... **SOURCE OF ANXIETY** ....

PHYSICAL SENSATIONS ....

NEGATIVE BELIEVES

ABOUT SITUATION ....
....

ABOUT YOUSELF ....
....

WHAT FACTS DO YOU KNOW ARE TRUE?

ABOUT SITUATION ....
....

ABOUT YOUSELF ....
....

WHAT HAPPENED?

....
....

HOW DID IT MAKE YOU FEEL?

....
....

HOW DID YOU REACT?

....
....

WHAT HELPS YOU SOOTHE YOUR ANXIETY?

....
....

Anxiety Journal

DATE   TIME

PLACE   SOURCE OF ANXIETY

PHYSICAL SENSATIONS

NEGATIVE BELIEVES

ABOUT SITUATION ....
....

ABOUT YOUSELF ....
....

WHAT FACTS DO YOU KNOW ARE TRUE?

ABOUT SITUATION ....
....

ABOUT YOUSELF ....
....

WHAT HAPPENED?

....
....

HOW DID IT MAKE YOU FEEL?

....
....

HOW DID YOU REACT?

....
....

WHAT HELPS YOU SOOTHE YOUR ANXIETY?

....
....

DATE .... TIME ....

PLACE .... SOURCE OF ANXIETY ....

PHYSICAL SENSATIONS ....

NEGATIVE BELIEVES

ABOUT SITUATION ....
....

ABOUT YOUSELF ....
....

WHAT FACTS DO YOU KNOW ARE TRUE?

ABOUT SITUATION ....
....

ABOUT YOUSELF ....
....

WHAT HAPPENED?

....
....

HOW DID IT MAKE YOU FEEL?

....
....

HOW DID YOU REACT?

....
....

WHAT HELPS YOU SOOTHE YOUR ANXIETY?

....
....

DATE TIME

PLACE SOURCE OF ANXIETY

PHYSICAL SENSATIONS

NEGATIVE BELIEVES

ABOUT SITUATION ....
....

ABOUT YOUSELF ....
....

WHAT FACTS DO YOU KNOW ARE TRUE?

ABOUT SITUATION ....
....

ABOUT YOUSELF ....
....

WHAT HAPPENED?

....
....

HOW DID IT MAKE YOU FEEL?

....
....

HOW DID YOU REACT?

....
....

WHAT HELPS YOU SOOTHE YOUR ANXIETY?

....
....

Anxiety Journal

DATE .... **TIME** ....

PLACE .... **SOURCE OF ANXIETY** ....

PHYSICAL SENSATIONS ....

NEGATIVE BELIEVES

ABOUT SITUATION ....
....

ABOUT YOUSELF ....
....

WHAT FACTS DO YOU KNOW ARE TRUE?

ABOUT SITUATION ....
....

ABOUT YOUSELF ....
....

WHAT HAPPENED?

....
....

HOW DID IT MAKE YOU FEEL?

....
....

HOW DID YOU REACT?

....
....

WHAT HELPS YOU SOOTHE YOUR ANXIETY?

....
....

Anxiety Journal

DATE   TIME

PLACE   SOURCE OF ANXIETY

PHYSICAL SENSATIONS

NEGATIVE BELIEVES

ABOUT SITUATION ....
....

ABOUT YOUSELF ....
....

WHAT FACTS DO YOU KNOW ARE TRUE?

ABOUT SITUATION ....
....

ABOUT YOUSELF ....
....

WHAT HAPPENED?

....
....

HOW DID IT MAKE YOU FEEL?

....
....

HOW DID YOU REACT?

....
....

WHAT HELPS YOU SOOTHE YOUR ANXIETY?

....
....

Anxiety Journal

DATE .... TIME ....

PLACE .... SOURCE OF ANXIETY ....

PHYSICAL SENSATIONS ....

NEGATIVE BELIEVES

ABOUT SITUATION ....
....

ABOUT YOUSELF ....
....

WHAT FACTS DO YOU KNOW ARE TRUE?

ABOUT SITUATION ....
....

ABOUT YOUSELF ....
....

WHAT HAPPENED?

....
....

HOW DID IT MAKE YOU FEEL?

....
....

HOW DID YOU REACT?

....
....

WHAT HELPS YOU SOOTHE YOUR ANXIETY?

....
....

Anxiety Journal

DATE　　　　　　　　　　　　TIME

PLACE　　　　　　　　　　　SOURCE OF ANXIETY

PHYSICAL SENSATIONS

NEGATIVE BELIEVES

ABOUT SITUATION ....
....

ABOUT YOUSELF ....
....

WHAT FACTS DO YOU KNOW ARE TRUE?

ABOUT SITUATION ....
....

ABOUT YOUSELF ....
....

WHAT HAPPENED?

....
....

HOW DID IT MAKE YOU FEEL?

....
....

HOW DID YOU REACT?

....
....

WHAT HELPS YOU SOOTHE YOUR ANXIETY?

....
....

Anxiety Journal

DATE _____ **TIME** _____

PLACE _____ **SOURCE OF ANXIETY** _____

PHYSICAL SENSATIONS _____

NEGATIVE BELIEVES

ABOUT SITUATION ....
....

ABOUT YOUSELF ....
....

WHAT FACTS DO YOU KNOW ARE TRUE?

ABOUT SITUATION ....
....

ABOUT YOUSELF ....
....

WHAT HAPPENED?

....
....

HOW DID IT MAKE YOU FEEL?

....
....

HOW DID YOU REACT?

....
....

WHAT HELPS YOU SOOTHE YOUR ANXIETY?

....
....

Anxiety Journal

DATE   TIME

PLACE   SOURCE OF ANXIETY

PHYSICAL SENSATIONS

NEGATIVE BELIEVES

ABOUT SITUATION ....
....

ABOUT YOUSELF ....
....

WHAT FACTS DO YOU KNOW ARE TRUE?

ABOUT SITUATION ....
....

ABOUT YOUSELF ....
....

WHAT HAPPENED?

....
....

HOW DID IT MAKE YOU FEEL?

....
....

HOW DID YOU REACT?

....
....

WHAT HELPS YOU SOOTHE YOUR ANXIETY?

....
....

DATE _____ TIME _____
PLACE _____ SOURCE OF ANXIETY _____
PHYSICAL SENSATIONS _____

NEGATIVE BELIEVES

ABOUT SITUATION ....
....
ABOUT YOUSELF ....
....

WHAT FACTS DO YOU KNOW ARE TRUE?

ABOUT SITUATION ....
....
ABOUT YOUSELF ....
....

WHAT HAPPENED?

....
....

HOW DID IT MAKE YOU FEEL?

....
....

HOW DID YOU REACT?

....
....

WHAT HELPS YOU SOOTHE YOUR ANXIETY?

....
....

DATE   TIME

PLACE   SOURCE OF ANXIETY

PHYSICAL SENSATIONS

NEGATIVE BELIEVES

ABOUT SITUATION ....
....

ABOUT YOUSELF ....
....

WHAT FACTS DO YOU KNOW ARE TRUE?

ABOUT SITUATION ....
....

ABOUT YOUSELF ....
....

WHAT HAPPENED?

....
....

HOW DID IT MAKE YOU FEEL?

....
....

HOW DID YOU REACT?

....
....

WHAT HELPS YOU SOOTHE YOUR ANXIETY?

....
....

Anxiety Journal

DATE .... **TIME** ....
PLACE .... **SOURCE OF ANXIETY** ....
PHYSICAL SENSATIONS ....

NEGATIVE BELIEVES

ABOUT SITUATION ....
....
ABOUT YOUSELF ....
....

WHAT FACTS DO YOU KNOW ARE TRUE?

ABOUT SITUATION ....
....
ABOUT YOUSELF ....
....

WHAT HAPPENED?

....
....

HOW DID IT MAKE YOU FEEL?

....
....

HOW DID YOU REACT?

....
....

WHAT HELPS YOU SOOTHE YOUR ANXIETY?

....
....

DATE   TIME

PLACE   SOURCE OF ANXIETY

PHYSICAL SENSATIONS

NEGATIVE BELIEVES

ABOUT SITUATION ....
....

ABOUT YOUSELF ....
....

WHAT FACTS DO YOU KNOW ARE TRUE?

ABOUT SITUATION ....
....

ABOUT YOUSELF ....
....

WHAT HAPPENED?

....
....

HOW DID IT MAKE YOU FEEL?

....
....

HOW DID YOU REACT?

....
....

WHAT HELPS YOU SOOTHE YOUR ANXIETY?

....
....

Anxiety Journal

DATE .... TIME ....

PLACE .... SOURCE OF ANXIETY ....

PHYSICAL SENSATIONS ....

NEGATIVE BELIEVES

ABOUT SITUATION ....
....

ABOUT YOUSELF ....
....

WHAT FACTS DO YOU KNOW ARE TRUE?

ABOUT SITUATION ....
....

ABOUT YOUSELF ....
....

WHAT HAPPENED?

....
....

HOW DID IT MAKE YOU FEEL?

....
....

HOW DID YOU REACT?

....
....

WHAT HELPS YOU SOOTHE YOUR ANXIETY?

....
....

Anxiety Journal

DATE								TIME

PLACE							SOURCE OF ANXIETY

PHYSICAL SENSATIONS

NEGATIVE BELIEVES

ABOUT SITUATION ....
....

ABOUT YOUSELF ....
....

WHAT FACTS DO YOU KNOW ARE TRUE?

ABOUT SITUATION ....
....

ABOUT YOUSELF ....
....

WHAT HAPPENED?

....
....

HOW DID IT MAKE YOU FEEL?

....
....

HOW DID YOU REACT?

....
....

WHAT HELPS YOU SOOTHE YOUR ANXIETY?

....
....

Anxiety Journal

DATE .... **TIME** ....

PLACE .... **SOURCE OF ANXIETY** ....

PHYSICAL SENSATIONS ....

NEGATIVE BELIEVES

ABOUT SITUATION ....
....

ABOUT YOUSELF ....
....

WHAT FACTS DO YOU KNOW ARE TRUE?

ABOUT SITUATION ....
....

ABOUT YOUSELF ....
....

WHAT HAPPENED?

....
....

HOW DID IT MAKE YOU FEEL?

....
....

HOW DID YOU REACT?

....
....

WHAT HELPS YOU SOOTHE YOUR ANXIETY?

....
....

DATE   TIME

PLACE   SOURCE OF ANXIETY

PHYSICAL SENSATIONS

NEGATIVE BELIEVES

ABOUT SITUATION ....
....

ABOUT YOUSELF ....
....

WHAT FACTS DO YOU KNOW ARE TRUE?

ABOUT SITUATION ....
....

ABOUT YOUSELF ....
....

WHAT HAPPENED?

....
....

HOW DID IT MAKE YOU FEEL?

....
....

HOW DID YOU REACT?

....
....

WHAT HELPS YOU SOOTHE YOUR ANXIETY?

....
....

DATE .... TIME ....
PLACE .... SOURCE OF ANXIETY ....
PHYSICAL SENSATIONS ....

NEGATIVE BELIEVES

ABOUT SITUATION ....
....

ABOUT YOUSELF ....
....

WHAT FACTS DO YOU KNOW ARE TRUE?

ABOUT SITUATION ....
....

ABOUT YOUSELF ....
....

WHAT HAPPENED?

....
....

HOW DID IT MAKE YOU FEEL?

....
....

HOW DID YOU REACT?

....
....

WHAT HELPS YOU SOOTHE YOUR ANXIETY?

....
....

Anxiety Journal

DATE   TIME

PLACE   SOURCE OF ANXIETY

PHYSICAL SENSATIONS

NEGATIVE BELIEVES

ABOUT SITUATION ....
....
ABOUT YOUSELF ....
....

WHAT FACTS DO YOU KNOW ARE TRUE?

ABOUT SITUATION ....
....
ABOUT YOUSELF ....
....

WHAT HAPPENED?

....
....

HOW DID IT MAKE YOU FEEL?

....
....

HOW DID YOU REACT?

....
....

WHAT HELPS YOU SOOTHE YOUR ANXIETY?

....
....

DATE .... TIME ....
PLACE .... SOURCE OF ANXIETY ....
PHYSICAL SENSATIONS ....

NEGATIVE BELIEVES

ABOUT SITUATION ....
....
ABOUT YOUSELF ....
....

WHAT FACTS DO YOU KNOW ARE TRUE?

ABOUT SITUATION ....
....
ABOUT YOUSELF ....
....

WHAT HAPPENED?

....
....

HOW DID IT MAKE YOU FEEL?

....
....

HOW DID YOU REACT?

....
....

WHAT HELPS YOU SOOTHE YOUR ANXIETY?

....
....

Anxiety Journal

DATE   TIME

PLACE   SOURCE OF ANXIETY

PHYSICAL SENSATIONS

NEGATIVE BELIEVES

ABOUT SITUATION ....
....

ABOUT YOUSELF ....
....

WHAT FACTS DO YOU KNOW ARE TRUE?

ABOUT SITUATION ....
....

ABOUT YOUSELF ....
....

WHAT HAPPENED?

....
....

HOW DID IT MAKE YOU FEEL?

....
....

HOW DID YOU REACT?

....
....

WHAT HELPS YOU SOOTHE YOUR ANXIETY?

....
....

DATE _____ **TIME** _____

PLACE _____ **SOURCE OF ANXIETY** _____

PHYSICAL SENSATIONS _____

NEGATIVE BELIEVES

ABOUT SITUATION ....
....

ABOUT YOUSELF ....
....

WHAT FACTS DO YOU KNOW ARE TRUE?

ABOUT SITUATION ....
....

ABOUT YOUSELF ....
....

WHAT HAPPENED?

....
....

HOW DID IT MAKE YOU FEEL?

....
....

HOW DID YOU REACT?

....
....

WHAT HELPS YOU SOOTHE YOUR ANXIETY?

....
....

Anxiety Journal

DATE   TIME

PLACE   SOURCE OF ANXIETY

PHYSICAL SENSATIONS

NEGATIVE BELIEVES

ABOUT SITUATION ....
....

ABOUT YOUSELF ....
....

WHAT FACTS DO YOU KNOW ARE TRUE?

ABOUT SITUATION ....
....

ABOUT YOUSELF ....
....

WHAT HAPPENED?

....
....

HOW DID IT MAKE YOU FEEL?

....
....

HOW DID YOU REACT?

....
....

WHAT HELPS YOU SOOTHE YOUR ANXIETY?

....
....

Anxiety Journal

DATE _____ TIME _____

PLACE _____ SOURCE OF ANXIETY _____

PHYSICAL SENSATIONS _____

NEGATIVE BELIEVES

ABOUT SITUATION ....
....

ABOUT YOUSELF ....
....

WHAT FACTS DO YOU KNOW ARE TRUE?

ABOUT SITUATION ....
....

ABOUT YOUSELF ....
....

WHAT HAPPENED?

....
....

HOW DID IT MAKE YOU FEEL?

....
....

HOW DID YOU REACT?

....
....

WHAT HELPS YOU SOOTHE YOUR ANXIETY?

....
....

Anxiety Journal

DATE TIME

PLACE SOURCE OF ANXIETY

PHYSICAL SENSATIONS

NEGATIVE BELIEVES

ABOUT SITUATION ....
....

ABOUT YOUSELF ....
....

WHAT FACTS DO YOU KNOW ARE TRUE?

ABOUT SITUATION ....
....

ABOUT YOUSELF ....
....

WHAT HAPPENED?

....
....

HOW DID IT MAKE YOU FEEL?

....
....

HOW DID YOU REACT?

....
....

WHAT HELPS YOU SOOTHE YOUR ANXIETY?

....
....

Anxiety Journal

DATE .... **TIME** ....

PLACE .... **SOURCE OF ANXIETY** ....

PHYSICAL SENSATIONS ....

NEGATIVE BELIEVES

ABOUT SITUATION ....
....

ABOUT YOUSELF ....
....

WHAT FACTS DO YOU KNOW ARE TRUE?

ABOUT SITUATION ....
....

ABOUT YOUSELF ....
....

WHAT HAPPENED?
....
....

HOW DID IT MAKE YOU FEEL?
....
....

HOW DID YOU REACT?
....
....

WHAT HELPS YOU SOOTHE YOUR ANXIETY?
....
....

Anxiety Journal

DATE   TIME

PLACE   SOURCE OF ANXIETY

PHYSICAL SENSATIONS

NEGATIVE BELIEVES

ABOUT SITUATION ....
....

ABOUT YOUSELF ....
....

WHAT FACTS DO YOU KNOW ARE TRUE?

ABOUT SITUATION ....
....

ABOUT YOUSELF ....
....

WHAT HAPPENED?

....
....

HOW DID IT MAKE YOU FEEL?

....
....

HOW DID YOU REACT?

....
....

WHAT HELPS YOU SOOTHE YOUR ANXIETY?

....
....

Anxiety Journal

DATE　　　　　　　　　　　**TIME**

PLACE　　　　　　　**SOURCE OF ANXIETY**

PHYSICAL SENSATIONS

NEGATIVE BELIEVES

ABOUT SITUATION ....
....

ABOUT YOUSELF ....
....

WHAT FACTS DO YOU KNOW ARE TRUE?

ABOUT SITUATION ....
....

ABOUT YOUSELF ....
....

WHAT HAPPENED?

....
....

HOW DID IT MAKE YOU FEEL?

....
....

HOW DID YOU REACT?

....
....

WHAT HELPS YOU SOOTHE YOUR ANXIETY?

....
....

DATE TIME

PLACE SOURCE OF ANXIETY

PHYSICAL SENSATIONS

NEGATIVE BELIEVES

ABOUT SITUATION ....

ABOUT YOUSELF ....

WHAT FACTS DO YOU KNOW ARE TRUE?

ABOUT SITUATION ....

ABOUT YOUSELF ....

WHAT HAPPENED?

....

HOW DID IT MAKE YOU FEEL?

....

HOW DID YOU REACT?

....

WHAT HELPS YOU SOOTHE YOUR ANXIETY?

....

DATE TIME
PLACE SOURCE OF ANXIETY
PHYSICAL SENSATIONS

NEGATIVE BELIEVES

ABOUT SITUATION ....
....
ABOUT YOUSELF ....
....

WHAT FACTS DO YOU KNOW ARE TRUE?

ABOUT SITUATION ....
....
ABOUT YOUSELF ....
....

WHAT HAPPENED?

....
....

HOW DID IT MAKE YOU FEEL?

....
....

HOW DID YOU REACT?

....
....

WHAT HELPS YOU SOOTHE YOUR ANXIETY?

....
....

Anxiety Journal

DATE   TIME

PLACE   SOURCE OF ANXIETY

PHYSICAL SENSATIONS

NEGATIVE BELIEVES

ABOUT SITUATION ....
....
ABOUT YOUSELF ....
....

WHAT FACTS DO YOU KNOW ARE TRUE?

ABOUT SITUATION ....
....
ABOUT YOUSELF ....
....

WHAT HAPPENED?

....
....

HOW DID IT MAKE YOU FEEL?

....
....

HOW DID YOU REACT?

....
....

WHAT HELPS YOU SOOTHE YOUR ANXIETY?

....
....

Anxiety Journal

DATE _____ TIME _____

PLACE _____ SOURCE OF ANXIETY _____

PHYSICAL SENSATIONS _____

NEGATIVE BELIEVES

ABOUT SITUATION ....
....

ABOUT YOUSELF ....
....

WHAT FACTS DO YOU KNOW ARE TRUE?

ABOUT SITUATION ....
....

ABOUT YOUSELF ....
....

WHAT HAPPENED?

....
....

HOW DID IT MAKE YOU FEEL?

....
....

HOW DID YOU REACT?

....
....

WHAT HELPS YOU SOOTHE YOUR ANXIETY?

....
....

Anxiety Journal

DATE   TIME

PLACE   SOURCE OF ANXIETY

PHYSICAL SENSATIONS

NEGATIVE BELIEVES

ABOUT SITUATION ....
....

ABOUT YOUSELF ....
....

WHAT FACTS DO YOU KNOW ARE TRUE?

ABOUT SITUATION ....
....

ABOUT YOUSELF ....
....

WHAT HAPPENED?

....
....

HOW DID IT MAKE YOU FEEL?

....
....

HOW DID YOU REACT?

....
....

WHAT HELPS YOU SOOTHE YOUR ANXIETY?

....
....

Anxiety Journal

DATE _____ **TIME** _____

PLACE _____ **SOURCE OF ANXIETY** _____

PHYSICAL SENSATIONS _____

NEGATIVE BELIEVES

ABOUT SITUATION ....
....

ABOUT YOUSELF ....
....

WHAT FACTS DO YOU KNOW ARE TRUE?

ABOUT SITUATION ....
....

ABOUT YOUSELF ....
....

WHAT HAPPENED?

....
....

HOW DID IT MAKE YOU FEEL?

....
....

HOW DID YOU REACT?

....
....

WHAT HELPS YOU SOOTHE YOUR ANXIETY?

....
....

Anxiety Journal

DATE   TIME

PLACE   SOURCE OF ANXIETY

PHYSICAL SENSATIONS

NEGATIVE BELIEVES

ABOUT SITUATION ....
....

ABOUT YOUSELF ....
....

WHAT FACTS DO YOU KNOW ARE TRUE?

ABOUT SITUATION ....
....

ABOUT YOUSELF ....
....

WHAT HAPPENED?

....
....

HOW DID IT MAKE YOU FEEL?

....
....

HOW DID YOU REACT?

....
....

WHAT HELPS YOU SOOTHE YOUR ANXIETY?

....
....

Anxiety Journal

DATE .... **TIME** ....

PLACE .... **SOURCE OF ANXIETY** ....

PHYSICAL SENSATIONS ....

NEGATIVE BELIEVES

ABOUT SITUATION ....
....

ABOUT YOUSELF ....
....

WHAT FACTS DO YOU KNOW ARE TRUE?

ABOUT SITUATION ....
....

ABOUT YOUSELF ....
....

WHAT HAPPENED?

....
....

HOW DID IT MAKE YOU FEEL?

....
....

HOW DID YOU REACT?

....
....

WHAT HELPS YOU SOOTHE YOUR ANXIETY?

....
....

Anxiety Journal

DATE   TIME

PLACE   SOURCE OF ANXIETY

PHYSICAL SENSATIONS

NEGATIVE BELIEVES

ABOUT SITUATION ....
....

ABOUT YOUSELF ....
....

WHAT FACTS DO YOU KNOW ARE TRUE?

ABOUT SITUATION ....
....

ABOUT YOUSELF ....
....

WHAT HAPPENED?

....
....

HOW DID IT MAKE YOU FEEL?

....
....

HOW DID YOU REACT?

....
....

WHAT HELPS YOU SOOTHE YOUR ANXIETY?

....
....

Anxiety Journal

DATE .... **TIME** ....

PLACE .... **SOURCE OF ANXIETY** ....

PHYSICAL SENSATIONS ....

NEGATIVE BELIEVES

ABOUT SITUATION ....
....

ABOUT YOUSELF ....
....

WHAT FACTS DO YOU KNOW ARE TRUE?

ABOUT SITUATION ....
....

ABOUT YOUSELF ....
....

WHAT HAPPENED?
....
....

HOW DID IT MAKE YOU FEEL?
....
....

HOW DID YOU REACT?
....
....

WHAT HELPS YOU SOOTHE YOUR ANXIETY?
....
....

Anxiety Journal

DATE   TIME

PLACE   SOURCE OF ANXIETY

PHYSICAL SENSATIONS

NEGATIVE BELIEVES

ABOUT SITUATION ....
....

ABOUT YOUSELF ....
....

WHAT FACTS DO YOU KNOW ARE TRUE?

ABOUT SITUATION ....
....

ABOUT YOUSELF ....
....

WHAT HAPPENED?

....
....

HOW DID IT MAKE YOU FEEL?

....
....

HOW DID YOU REACT?

....
....

WHAT HELPS YOU SOOTHE YOUR ANXIETY?

....
....

Anxiety Journal

DATE _____ **TIME** _____

PLACE _____ **SOURCE OF ANXIETY** _____

PHYSICAL SENSATIONS _____

NEGATIVE BELIEVES

ABOUT SITUATION ....
....

ABOUT YOUSELF ....
....

WHAT FACTS DO YOU KNOW ARE TRUE?

ABOUT SITUATION ....
....

ABOUT YOUSELF ....
....

WHAT HAPPENED?

....
....

HOW DID IT MAKE YOU FEEL?

....
....

HOW DID YOU REACT?

....
....

WHAT HELPS YOU SOOTHE YOUR ANXIETY?

....
....

DATE   TIME

PLACE   SOURCE OF ANXIETY

PHYSICAL SENSATIONS

NEGATIVE BELIEVES

ABOUT SITUATION ....
....

ABOUT YOUSELF ....
....

WHAT FACTS DO YOU KNOW ARE TRUE?

ABOUT SITUATION ....
....

ABOUT YOUSELF ....
....

WHAT HAPPENED?

....
....

HOW DID IT MAKE YOU FEEL?

....
....

HOW DID YOU REACT?

....
....

WHAT HELPS YOU SOOTHE YOUR ANXIETY?

....
....

Anxiety Journal

DATE .... **TIME** ....

PLACE .... **SOURCE OF ANXIETY** ....

PHYSICAL SENSATIONS ....

NEGATIVE BELIEVES

ABOUT SITUATION ....
....

ABOUT YOUSELF ....
....

WHAT FACTS DO YOU KNOW ARE TRUE?

ABOUT SITUATION ....
....

ABOUT YOUSELF ....
....

WHAT HAPPENED?

....
....

HOW DID IT MAKE YOU FEEL?

....
....

HOW DID YOU REACT?

....
....

WHAT HELPS YOU SOOTHE YOUR ANXIETY?

....
....

Anxiety Journal

DATE   TIME

PLACE   SOURCE OF ANXIETY

PHYSICAL SENSATIONS

NEGATIVE BELIEVES

ABOUT SITUATION ....

ABOUT YOUSELF ....

WHAT FACTS DO YOU KNOW ARE TRUE?

ABOUT SITUATION ....

ABOUT YOUSELF ....

WHAT HAPPENED?

....

....

HOW DID IT MAKE YOU FEEL?

....

....

HOW DID YOU REACT?

....

....

WHAT HELPS YOU SOOTHE YOUR ANXIETY?

....

....

Anxiety Journal

DATE .... TIME ....
PLACE .... SOURCE OF ANXIETY ....
PHYSICAL SENSATIONS ....

NEGATIVE BELIEVES

ABOUT SITUATION ....
....
ABOUT YOUSELF ....
....

WHAT FACTS DO YOU KNOW ARE TRUE?

ABOUT SITUATION ....
....
ABOUT YOUSELF ....
....

WHAT HAPPENED?

....
....

HOW DID IT MAKE YOU FEEL?

....
....

HOW DID YOU REACT?

....
....

WHAT HELPS YOU SOOTHE YOUR ANXIETY?

....
....

Anxiety Journal

DATE .... TIME ....

PLACE .... SOURCE OF ANXIETY ....

PHYSICAL SENSATIONS ....

NEGATIVE BELIEVES

ABOUT SITUATION ....
....

ABOUT YOUSELF ....
....

WHAT FACTS DO YOU KNOW ARE TRUE?

ABOUT SITUATION ....
....

ABOUT YOUSELF ....
....

WHAT HAPPENED?

....
....

HOW DID IT MAKE YOU FEEL?

....
....

HOW DID YOU REACT?

....
....

WHAT HELPS YOU SOOTHE YOUR ANXIETY?

....
....

Anxiety Journal

DATE .... **TIME** ....

PLACE .... **SOURCE OF ANXIETY** ....

PHYSICAL SENSATIONS ....

NEGATIVE BELIEVES

ABOUT SITUATION ....
....

ABOUT YOUSELF ....
....

WHAT FACTS DO YOU KNOW ARE TRUE?

ABOUT SITUATION ....
....

ABOUT YOUSELF ....
....

WHAT HAPPENED?

....
....

HOW DID IT MAKE YOU FEEL?

....
....

HOW DID YOU REACT?

....
....

WHAT HELPS YOU SOOTHE YOUR ANXIETY?

....
....

Anxiety Journal

DATE **TIME**

PLACE **SOURCE OF ANXIETY**

PHYSICAL SENSATIONS

NEGATIVE BELIEVES

ABOUT SITUATION ....
....

ABOUT YOUSELF ....
....

WHAT FACTS DO YOU KNOW ARE TRUE?

ABOUT SITUATION ....
....

ABOUT YOUSELF ....
....

WHAT HAPPENED?

....
....

HOW DID IT MAKE YOU FEEL?

....
....

HOW DID YOU REACT?

....
....

WHAT HELPS YOU SOOTHE YOUR ANXIETY?

....
....

Anxiety Journal

DATE _____ TIME _____

PLACE _____ SOURCE OF ANXIETY _____

PHYSICAL SENSATIONS _____

NEGATIVE BELIEVES

ABOUT SITUATION ....
....

ABOUT YOUSELF ....
....

WHAT FACTS DO YOU KNOW ARE TRUE?

ABOUT SITUATION ....
....

ABOUT YOUSELF ....
....

WHAT HAPPENED?

....
....

HOW DID IT MAKE YOU FEEL?

....
....

HOW DID YOU REACT?

....
....

WHAT HELPS YOU SOOTHE YOUR ANXIETY?

....
....

Anxiety Journal

DATE   TIME

PLACE   SOURCE OF ANXIETY

PHYSICAL SENSATIONS

NEGATIVE BELIEVES

ABOUT SITUATION ....
....
ABOUT YOUSELF ....
....

WHAT FACTS DO YOU KNOW ARE TRUE?

ABOUT SITUATION ....
....
ABOUT YOUSELF ....
....

WHAT HAPPENED?

....
....

HOW DID IT MAKE YOU FEEL?

....
....

HOW DID YOU REACT?

....
....

WHAT HELPS YOU SOOTHE YOUR ANXIETY?

....
....

Anxiety Journal

DATE _____   TIME _____

PLACE _____   SOURCE OF ANXIETY _____

PHYSICAL SENSATIONS _____

NEGATIVE BELIEVES

ABOUT SITUATION ....
....

ABOUT YOUSELF ....
....

WHAT FACTS DO YOU KNOW ARE TRUE?

ABOUT SITUATION ....
....

ABOUT YOUSELF ....
....

WHAT HAPPENED?

....
....

HOW DID IT MAKE YOU FEEL?

....
....

HOW DID YOU REACT?

....
....

WHAT HELPS YOU SOOTHE YOUR ANXIETY?

....
....

Anxiety Journal

DATE   TIME

PLACE   SOURCE OF ANXIETY

PHYSICAL SENSATIONS

NEGATIVE BELIEVES

ABOUT SITUATION ....
....

ABOUT YOUSELF ....
....

WHAT FACTS DO YOU KNOW ARE TRUE?

ABOUT SITUATION ....
....

ABOUT YOUSELF ....
....

WHAT HAPPENED?

....
....

HOW DID IT MAKE YOU FEEL?

....
....

HOW DID YOU REACT?

....
....

WHAT HELPS YOU SOOTHE YOUR ANXIETY?

....
....

Anxiety Journal

DATE _____ **TIME** _____

PLACE _____ **SOURCE OF ANXIETY** _____

PHYSICAL SENSATIONS _____

NEGATIVE BELIEVES

ABOUT SITUATION ....
....

ABOUT YOUSELF ....
....

WHAT FACTS DO YOU KNOW ARE TRUE?

ABOUT SITUATION ....
....

ABOUT YOUSELF ....
....

WHAT HAPPENED?

....
....

HOW DID IT MAKE YOU FEEL?

....
....

HOW DID YOU REACT?

....
....

WHAT HELPS YOU SOOTHE YOUR ANXIETY?

....
....

Anxiety Journal

DATE   TIME

PLACE   SOURCE OF ANXIETY

PHYSICAL SENSATIONS

NEGATIVE BELIEVES

ABOUT SITUATION ....
....

ABOUT YOUSELF ....
....

WHAT FACTS DO YOU KNOW ARE TRUE?

ABOUT SITUATION ....
....

ABOUT YOUSELF ....
....

WHAT HAPPENED?

....
....

HOW DID IT MAKE YOU FEEL?

....
....

HOW DID YOU REACT?

....
....

WHAT HELPS YOU SOOTHE YOUR ANXIETY?

....
....

Anxiety Journal

DATE _____ **TIME** _____

PLACE _____ **SOURCE OF ANXIETY** _____

PHYSICAL SENSATIONS _____

NEGATIVE BELIEVES

ABOUT SITUATION ....
....

ABOUT YOUSELF ....
....

WHAT FACTS DO YOU KNOW ARE TRUE?

ABOUT SITUATION ....
....

ABOUT YOUSELF ....
....

WHAT HAPPENED?

....
....

HOW DID IT MAKE YOU FEEL?

....
....

HOW DID YOU REACT?

....
....

WHAT HELPS YOU SOOTHE YOUR ANXIETY?

....
....

DATE TIME

PLACE SOURCE OF ANXIETY

PHYSICAL SENSATIONS

NEGATIVE BELIEVES

ABOUT SITUATION ....

....

ABOUT YOUSELF ....

....

WHAT FACTS DO YOU KNOW ARE TRUE?

ABOUT SITUATION ....

....

ABOUT YOUSELF ....

....

WHAT HAPPENED?

....

....

HOW DID IT MAKE YOU FEEL?

....

....

HOW DID YOU REACT?

....

....

WHAT HELPS YOU SOOTHE YOUR ANXIETY?

....

....

Anxiety Journal

DATE _____ TIME _____

PLACE _____ SOURCE OF ANXIETY _____

PHYSICAL SENSATIONS _____

NEGATIVE BELIEVES

ABOUT SITUATION ....
....

ABOUT YOUSELF ....
....

WHAT FACTS DO YOU KNOW ARE TRUE?

ABOUT SITUATION ....
....

ABOUT YOUSELF ....
....

WHAT HAPPENED?

....
....

HOW DID IT MAKE YOU FEEL?

....
....

HOW DID YOU REACT?

....
....

WHAT HELPS YOU SOOTHE YOUR ANXIETY?

....
....

Anxiety Journal

DATE   TIME

PLACE   SOURCE OF ANXIETY

PHYSICAL SENSATIONS

NEGATIVE BELIEVES

ABOUT SITUATION ....

....

ABOUT YOUSELF ....

....

WHAT FACTS DO YOU KNOW ARE TRUE?

ABOUT SITUATION ....

....

ABOUT YOUSELF ....

....

WHAT HAPPENED?

....

....

HOW DID IT MAKE YOU FEEL?

....

....

HOW DID YOU REACT?

....

....

WHAT HELPS YOU SOOTHE YOUR ANXIETY?

....

....

Anxiety Journal

DATE   **TIME**

PLACE   **SOURCE OF ANXIETY**

PHYSICAL SENSATIONS

NEGATIVE BELIEVES

ABOUT SITUATION ....
....

ABOUT YOUSELF ....
....

WHAT FACTS DO YOU KNOW ARE TRUE?

ABOUT SITUATION ....
....

ABOUT YOUSELF ....
....

WHAT HAPPENED?

....
....

HOW DID IT MAKE YOU FEEL?

....
....

HOW DID YOU REACT?

....
....

WHAT HELPS YOU SOOTHE YOUR ANXIETY?

....
....

DATE   TIME

PLACE   SOURCE OF ANXIETY

PHYSICAL SENSATIONS

NEGATIVE BELIEVES

ABOUT SITUATION ....
....

ABOUT YOUSELF ....
....

WHAT FACTS DO YOU KNOW ARE TRUE?

ABOUT SITUATION ....
....

ABOUT YOUSELF ....
....

WHAT HAPPENED?

....
....

HOW DID IT MAKE YOU FEEL?

....
....

HOW DID YOU REACT?

....
....

WHAT HELPS YOU SOOTHE YOUR ANXIETY?

....
....

Anxiety Journal

DATE .... **TIME** ....

PLACE .... **SOURCE OF ANXIETY** ....

PHYSICAL SENSATIONS ....

NEGATIVE BELIEVES

ABOUT SITUATION ....
....

ABOUT YOUSELF ....
....

WHAT FACTS DO YOU KNOW ARE TRUE?

ABOUT SITUATION ....
....

ABOUT YOUSELF ....
....

WHAT HAPPENED?

....
....

HOW DID IT MAKE YOU FEEL?

....
....

HOW DID YOU REACT?

....
....

WHAT HELPS YOU SOOTHE YOUR ANXIETY?

....
....

Anxiety Journal

DATE   TIME

PLACE   SOURCE OF ANXIETY

PHYSICAL SENSATIONS

NEGATIVE BELIEVES

ABOUT SITUATION ....
....

ABOUT YOUSELF ....
....

WHAT FACTS DO YOU KNOW ARE TRUE?

ABOUT SITUATION ....
....

ABOUT YOUSELF ....
....

WHAT HAPPENED?

....
....

HOW DID IT MAKE YOU FEEL?

....
....

HOW DID YOU REACT?

....
....

WHAT HELPS YOU SOOTHE YOUR ANXIETY?

....
....

Anxiety Journal

DATE .... TIME ....

PLACE .... SOURCE OF ANXIETY ....

PHYSICAL SENSATIONS ....

NEGATIVE BELIEVES

ABOUT SITUATION ....
....

ABOUT YOUSELF ....
....

WHAT FACTS DO YOU KNOW ARE TRUE?

ABOUT SITUATION ....
....

ABOUT YOUSELF ....
....

WHAT HAPPENED?

....
....

HOW DID IT MAKE YOU FEEL?

....
....

HOW DID YOU REACT?

....
....

WHAT HELPS YOU SOOTHE YOUR ANXIETY?

....
....

Anxiety Journal

DATE   TIME

PLACE   SOURCE OF ANXIETY

PHYSICAL SENSATIONS

NEGATIVE BELIEVES

ABOUT SITUATION ....
....

ABOUT YOUSELF ....
....

WHAT FACTS DO YOU KNOW ARE TRUE?

ABOUT SITUATION ....
....

ABOUT YOUSELF ....
....

WHAT HAPPENED?

....
....

HOW DID IT MAKE YOU FEEL?

....
....

HOW DID YOU REACT?

....
....

WHAT HELPS YOU SOOTHE YOUR ANXIETY?

....
....

Anxiety Journal

DATE .... **TIME** ....

PLACE .... **SOURCE OF ANXIETY** ....

PHYSICAL SENSATIONS ....

NEGATIVE BELIEVES

ABOUT SITUATION ....
....

ABOUT YOURSELF ....
....

WHAT FACTS DO YOU KNOW ARE TRUE?

ABOUT SITUATION ....
....

ABOUT YOUSELF ....
....

WHAT HAPPENED?

....
....

HOW DID IT MAKE YOU FEEL?

....
....

HOW DID YOU REACT?

....
....

WHAT HELPS YOU SOOTHE YOUR ANXIETY?

....
....

DATE   TIME

PLACE   SOURCE OF ANXIETY

PHYSICAL SENSATIONS

NEGATIVE BELIEVES

ABOUT SITUATION ....
....

ABOUT YOUSELF ....
....

WHAT FACTS DO YOU KNOW ARE TRUE?

ABOUT SITUATION ....
....

ABOUT YOUSELF ....
....

WHAT HAPPENED?

....
....

HOW DID IT MAKE YOU FEEL?

....
....

HOW DID YOU REACT?

....
....

WHAT HELPS YOU SOOTHE YOUR ANXIETY?

....
....

Anxiety Journal

DATE   **TIME**

PLACE   **SOURCE OF ANXIETY**

PHYSICAL SENSATIONS

NEGATIVE BELIEVES

ABOUT SITUATION ....
....

ABOUT YOUSELF ....
....

WHAT FACTS DO YOU KNOW ARE TRUE?

ABOUT SITUATION ....
....

ABOUT YOUSELF ....
....

WHAT HAPPENED?

....
....

HOW DID IT MAKE YOU FEEL?

....
....

HOW DID YOU REACT?

....
....

WHAT HELPS YOU SOOTHE YOUR ANXIETY?

....
....

DATE   TIME

PLACE   SOURCE OF ANXIETY

PHYSICAL SENSATIONS

NEGATIVE BELIEVES

ABOUT SITUATION ....
....

ABOUT YOUSELF ....
....

WHAT FACTS DO YOU KNOW ARE TRUE?

ABOUT SITUATION ....
....

ABOUT YOUSELF ....
....

WHAT HAPPENED?

....
....

HOW DID IT MAKE YOU FEEL?

....
....

HOW DID YOU REACT?

....
....

WHAT HELPS YOU SOOTHE YOUR ANXIETY?

....
....

Anxiety Journal

DATE .... **TIME** ....

PLACE .... **SOURCE OF ANXIETY** ....

PHYSICAL SENSATIONS ....

NEGATIVE BELIEVES

ABOUT SITUATION ....
....

ABOUT YOUSELF ....
....

WHAT FACTS DO YOU KNOW ARE TRUE?

ABOUT SITUATION ....
....

ABOUT YOUSELF ....
....

WHAT HAPPENED?

....
....

HOW DID IT MAKE YOU FEEL?

....
....

HOW DID YOU REACT?

....
....

WHAT HELPS YOU SOOTHE YOUR ANXIETY?

....
....

DATE   TIME

PLACE   SOURCE OF ANXIETY

PHYSICAL SENSATIONS

NEGATIVE BELIEVES

ABOUT SITUATION ....

....

ABOUT YOUSELF ....

....

WHAT FACTS DO YOU KNOW ARE TRUE?

ABOUT SITUATION ....

....

ABOUT YOUSELF ....

....

WHAT HAPPENED?

....

....

HOW DID IT MAKE YOU FEEL?

....

....

HOW DID YOU REACT?

....

....

WHAT HELPS YOU SOOTHE YOUR ANXIETY?

....

....

DATE   **TIME**

PLACE   **SOURCE OF ANXIETY**

PHYSICAL SENSATIONS

NEGATIVE BELIEVES

ABOUT SITUATION ....
....

ABOUT YOUSELF ....
....

WHAT FACTS DO YOU KNOW ARE TRUE?

ABOUT SITUATION ....
....

ABOUT YOUSELF ....
....

WHAT HAPPENED?

....
....

HOW DID IT MAKE YOU FEEL?

....
....

HOW DID YOU REACT?

....
....

WHAT HELPS YOU SOOTHE YOUR ANXIETY?

....
....

DATE   TIME

PLACE   SOURCE OF ANXIETY

PHYSICAL SENSATIONS

NEGATIVE BELIEVES

ABOUT SITUATION ....
....

ABOUT YOUSELF ....
....

WHAT FACTS DO YOU KNOW ARE TRUE?

ABOUT SITUATION ....
....

ABOUT YOUSELF ....
....

WHAT HAPPENED?

....
....

HOW DID IT MAKE YOU FEEL?

....
....

HOW DID YOU REACT?

....
....

WHAT HELPS YOU SOOTHE YOUR ANXIETY?

....
....

Anxiety Journal

DATE   **TIME**

PLACE   **SOURCE OF ANXIETY**

PHYSICAL SENSATIONS

NEGATIVE BELIEVES

ABOUT SITUATION ....
....

ABOUT YOUSELF ....
....

WHAT FACTS DO YOU KNOW ARE TRUE?

ABOUT SITUATION ....
....

ABOUT YOUSELF ....
....

WHAT HAPPENED?

....
....

HOW DID IT MAKE YOU FEEL?

....
....

HOW DID YOU REACT?

....
....

WHAT HELPS YOU SOOTHE YOUR ANXIETY?

....
....

DATE   TIME

PLACE   SOURCE OF ANXIETY

PHYSICAL SENSATIONS

NEGATIVE BELIEVES

ABOUT SITUATION ....
....

ABOUT YOUSELF ....
....

WHAT FACTS DO YOU KNOW ARE TRUE?

ABOUT SITUATION ....
....

ABOUT YOUSELF ....
....

WHAT HAPPENED?

....
....

HOW DID IT MAKE YOU FEEL?

....
....

HOW DID YOU REACT?

....
....

WHAT HELPS YOU SOOTHE YOUR ANXIETY?

....
....

DATE .... TIME ....
PLACE .... SOURCE OF ANXIETY ....
PHYSICAL SENSATIONS ....

NEGATIVE BELIEVES

ABOUT SITUATION ....
....

ABOUT YOUSELF ....
....

WHAT FACTS DO YOU KNOW ARE TRUE?

ABOUT SITUATION ....
....

ABOUT YOUSELF ....
....

WHAT HAPPENED?

....
....

HOW DID IT MAKE YOU FEEL?

....
....

HOW DID YOU REACT?

....
....

WHAT HELPS YOU SOOTHE YOUR ANXIETY?

....
....

Anxiety Journal

DATE   TIME

PLACE   SOURCE OF ANXIETY

PHYSICAL SENSATIONS

NEGATIVE BELIEVES

ABOUT SITUATION ....
....

ABOUT YOUSELF ....
....

WHAT FACTS DO YOU KNOW ARE TRUE?

ABOUT SITUATION ....
....

ABOUT YOUSELF ....
....

WHAT HAPPENED?

....
....

HOW DID IT MAKE YOU FEEL?

....
....

HOW DID YOU REACT?

....
....

WHAT HELPS YOU SOOTHE YOUR ANXIETY?

....
....

Anxiety Journal

DATE _____ **TIME** _____

PLACE _____ **SOURCE OF ANXIETY** _____

PHYSICAL SENSATIONS _____

NEGATIVE BELIEVES

ABOUT SITUATION ....
....

ABOUT YOUSELF ....
....

WHAT FACTS DO YOU KNOW ARE TRUE?

ABOUT SITUATION ....
....

ABOUT YOUSELF ....
....

WHAT HAPPENED?

....
....

HOW DID IT MAKE YOU FEEL?

....
....

HOW DID YOU REACT?

....
....

WHAT HELPS YOU SOOTHE YOUR ANXIETY?

....
....

Anxiety Journal

DATE   TIME

PLACE   SOURCE OF ANXIETY

PHYSICAL SENSATIONS

NEGATIVE BELIEVES

ABOUT SITUATION ....
....

ABOUT YOUSELF ....
....

WHAT FACTS DO YOU KNOW ARE TRUE?

ABOUT SITUATION ....
....

ABOUT YOUSELF ....
....

WHAT HAPPENED?

....
....

HOW DID IT MAKE YOU FEEL?

....
....

HOW DID YOU REACT?

....
....

WHAT HELPS YOU SOOTHE YOUR ANXIETY?

....
....

DATE .... TIME ....

PLACE .... SOURCE OF ANXIETY ....

PHYSICAL SENSATIONS ....

NEGATIVE BELIEVES

ABOUT SITUATION ....
....

ABOUT YOUSELF ....
....

WHAT FACTS DO YOU KNOW ARE TRUE?

ABOUT SITUATION ....
....

ABOUT YOUSELF ....
....

WHAT HAPPENED?

....
....

HOW DID IT MAKE YOU FEEL?

....
....

HOW DID YOU REACT?

....
....

WHAT HELPS YOU SOOTHE YOUR ANXIETY?

....
....

Anxiety Journal

DATE   TIME

PLACE   SOURCE OF ANXIETY

PHYSICAL SENSATIONS

NEGATIVE BELIEVES

ABOUT SITUATION ....
....

ABOUT YOUSELF ....
....

WHAT FACTS DO YOU KNOW ARE TRUE?

ABOUT SITUATION ....
....

ABOUT YOUSELF ....
....

WHAT HAPPENED?

....
....

HOW DID IT MAKE YOU FEEL?

....
....

HOW DID YOU REACT?

....
....

WHAT HELPS YOU SOOTHE YOUR ANXIETY?

....
....

Anxiety Journal

DATE _____ TIME _____
PLACE _____ SOURCE OF ANXIETY _____
PHYSICAL SENSATIONS _____

NEGATIVE BELIEVES

ABOUT SITUATION ....
....
ABOUT YOURSELF ....
....

WHAT FACTS DO YOU KNOW ARE TRUE?

ABOUT SITUATION ....
....
ABOUT YOUSELF ....
....

WHAT HAPPENED?

....
....

HOW DID IT MAKE YOU FEEL?

....
....

HOW DID YOU REACT?

....
....

WHAT HELPS YOU SOOTHE YOUR ANXIETY?

....
....

Anxiety Journal

DATE   TIME

PLACE   SOURCE OF ANXIETY

PHYSICAL SENSATIONS

NEGATIVE BELIEVES

ABOUT SITUATION ....
....

ABOUT YOUSELF ....
....

WHAT FACTS DO YOU KNOW ARE TRUE?

ABOUT SITUATION ....
....

ABOUT YOUSELF ....
....

WHAT HAPPENED?

....
....

HOW DID IT MAKE YOU FEEL?

....
....

HOW DID YOU REACT?

....
....

WHAT HELPS YOU SOOTHE YOUR ANXIETY?

....
....

Anxiety Journal

DATE .... **TIME** ....

PLACE .... **SOURCE OF ANXIETY** ....

PHYSICAL SENSATIONS ....

NEGATIVE BELIEVES

ABOUT SITUATION ....
....

ABOUT YOUSELF ....
....

WHAT FACTS DO YOU KNOW ARE TRUE?

ABOUT SITUATION ....
....

ABOUT YOUSELF ....
....

WHAT HAPPENED?
....
....

HOW DID IT MAKE YOU FEEL?
....
....

HOW DID YOU REACT?
....
....

WHAT HELPS YOU SOOTHE YOUR ANXIETY?
....
....

Anxiety Journal

DATE   TIME

PLACE   SOURCE OF ANXIETY

PHYSICAL SENSATIONS

NEGATIVE BELIEVES

ABOUT SITUATION ....

....

ABOUT YOUSELF ....

....

WHAT FACTS DO YOU KNOW ARE TRUE?

ABOUT SITUATION ....

....

ABOUT YOUSELF ....

....

WHAT HAPPENED?

....

....

HOW DID IT MAKE YOU FEEL?

....

....

HOW DID YOU REACT?

....

....

WHAT HELPS YOU SOOTHE YOUR ANXIETY?

....

....

Anxiety Journal

DATE **TIME**

PLACE **SOURCE OF ANXIETY**

PHYSICAL SENSATIONS

NEGATIVE BELIEVES

ABOUT SITUATION ....
....

ABOUT YOUSELF ....
....

WHAT FACTS DO YOU KNOW ARE TRUE?

ABOUT SITUATION ....
....

ABOUT YOUSELF ....
....

WHAT HAPPENED?

....
....

HOW DID IT MAKE YOU FEEL?

....
....

HOW DID YOU REACT?

....
....

WHAT HELPS YOU SOOTHE YOUR ANXIETY?

....
....

Anxiety Journal

DATE TIME

PLACE SOURCE OF ANXIETY

PHYSICAL SENSATIONS

NEGATIVE BELIEVES

ABOUT SITUATION ....
....

ABOUT YOUSELF ....
....

WHAT FACTS DO YOU KNOW ARE TRUE?

ABOUT SITUATION ....
....

ABOUT YOUSELF ....
....

WHAT HAPPENED?

....
....

HOW DID IT MAKE YOU FEEL?

....
....

HOW DID YOU REACT?

....
....

WHAT HELPS YOU SOOTHE YOUR ANXIETY?

....
....

Anxiety Journal

DATE _____ **TIME** _____

PLACE _____ **SOURCE OF ANXIETY** _____

PHYSICAL SENSATIONS _____

NEGATIVE BELIEVES

ABOUT SITUATION ....
....

ABOUT YOUSELF ....
....

WHAT FACTS DO YOU KNOW ARE TRUE?

ABOUT SITUATION ....
....

ABOUT YOUSELF ....
....

WHAT HAPPENED?

....
....

HOW DID IT MAKE YOU FEEL?

....
....

HOW DID YOU REACT?

....
....

WHAT HELPS YOU SOOTHE YOUR ANXIETY?

....
....

Anxiety Journal

DATE   TIME

PLACE   SOURCE OF ANXIETY

PHYSICAL SENSATIONS

NEGATIVE BELIEVES

ABOUT SITUATION ....
....

ABOUT YOUSELF ....
....

WHAT FACTS DO YOU KNOW ARE TRUE?

ABOUT SITUATION ....
....

ABOUT YOUSELF ....
....

WHAT HAPPENED?

....
....

HOW DID IT MAKE YOU FEEL?

....
....

HOW DID YOU REACT?

....
....

WHAT HELPS YOU SOOTHE YOUR ANXIETY?

....
....

Anxiety Journal

DATE .... **TIME** ....

PLACE .... **SOURCE OF ANXIETY** ....

PHYSICAL SENSATIONS ....

NEGATIVE BELIEVES

ABOUT SITUATION ....
....

ABOUT YOUSELF ....
....

WHAT FACTS DO YOU KNOW ARE TRUE?

ABOUT SITUATION ....
....

ABOUT YOUSELF ....
....

WHAT HAPPENED?

....
....

HOW DID IT MAKE YOU FEEL?

....
....

HOW DID YOU REACT?

....
....

WHAT HELPS YOU SOOTHE YOUR ANXIETY?

....
....

Anxiety Journal

DATE					TIME

PLACE					SOURCE OF ANXIETY

PHYSICAL SENSATIONS

NEGATIVE BELIEVES

ABOUT SITUATION ....

....

ABOUT YOUSELF ....

....

WHAT FACTS DO YOU KNOW ARE TRUE?

ABOUT SITUATION ....

....

ABOUT YOUSELF ....

....

WHAT HAPPENED?

....

....

HOW DID IT MAKE YOU FEEL?

....

....

HOW DID YOU REACT?

....

....

WHAT HELPS YOU SOOTHE YOUR ANXIETY?

....

....

Anxiety Journal

DATE _____ **TIME** _____

PLACE _____ **SOURCE OF ANXIETY** _____

PHYSICAL SENSATIONS _____

NEGATIVE BELIEVES

ABOUT SITUATION ....
....

ABOUT YOUSELF ....
....

WHAT FACTS DO YOU KNOW ARE TRUE?

ABOUT SITUATION ....
....

ABOUT YOUSELF ....
....

WHAT HAPPENED?

....
....

HOW DID IT MAKE YOU FEEL?

....
....

HOW DID YOU REACT?

....
....

WHAT HELPS YOU SOOTHE YOUR ANXIETY?

....
....

Anxiety Journal

DATE   TIME

PLACE   SOURCE OF ANXIETY

PHYSICAL SENSATIONS

NEGATIVE BELIEVES

ABOUT SITUATION ....
....

ABOUT YOUSELF ....
....

WHAT FACTS DO YOU KNOW ARE TRUE?

ABOUT SITUATION ....
....

ABOUT YOUSELF ....
....

WHAT HAPPENED?

....
....

HOW DID IT MAKE YOU FEEL?

....
....

HOW DID YOU REACT?

....
....

WHAT HELPS YOU SOOTHE YOUR ANXIETY?

....
....

Anxiety Journal

DATE _____ TIME _____

PLACE _____ SOURCE OF ANXIETY _____

PHYSICAL SENSATIONS _____

NEGATIVE BELIEVES

ABOUT SITUATION ....
....

ABOUT YOUSELF ....
....

WHAT FACTS DO YOU KNOW ARE TRUE?

ABOUT SITUATION ....
....

ABOUT YOUSELF ....
....

WHAT HAPPENED?

....
....

HOW DID IT MAKE YOU FEEL?

....
....

HOW DID YOU REACT?

....
....

WHAT HELPS YOU SOOTHE YOUR ANXIETY?

....
....

DATE   TIME

PLACE   SOURCE OF ANXIETY

PHYSICAL SENSATIONS

NEGATIVE BELIEVES

ABOUT SITUATION ....
....

ABOUT YOUSELF ....
....

WHAT FACTS DO YOU KNOW ARE TRUE?

ABOUT SITUATION ....
....

ABOUT YOUSELF ....
....

WHAT HAPPENED?

....
....

HOW DID IT MAKE YOU FEEL?

....
....

HOW DID YOU REACT?

....
....

WHAT HELPS YOU SOOTHE YOUR ANXIETY?

....
....

Anxiety Journal

DATE: _____ TIME: _____

PLACE: _____ SOURCE OF ANXIETY: _____

PHYSICAL SENSATIONS: _____

NEGATIVE BELIEVES

ABOUT SITUATION ....
....

ABOUT YOUSELF ....
....

WHAT FACTS DO YOU KNOW ARE TRUE?

ABOUT SITUATION ....
....

ABOUT YOUSELF ....
....

WHAT HAPPENED?

....
....

HOW DID IT MAKE YOU FEEL?

....
....

HOW DID YOU REACT?

....
....

WHAT HELPS YOU SOOTHE YOUR ANXIETY?

....
....

Anxiety Journal

DATE   TIME

PLACE   SOURCE OF ANXIETY

PHYSICAL SENSATIONS

NEGATIVE BELIEVES

ABOUT SITUATION ....
....

ABOUT YOUSELF ....
....

WHAT FACTS DO YOU KNOW ARE TRUE?

ABOUT SITUATION ....
....

ABOUT YOUSELF ....
....

WHAT HAPPENED?

....
....

HOW DID IT MAKE YOU FEEL?

....
....

HOW DID YOU REACT?

....
....

WHAT HELPS YOU SOOTHE YOUR ANXIETY?

....
....

Anxiety Journal

DATE **TIME**
PLACE **SOURCE OF ANXIETY**
PHYSICAL SENSATIONS

NEGATIVE BELIEVES

ABOUT SITUATION ....
....
ABOUT YOUSELF ....
....

WHAT FACTS DO YOU KNOW ARE TRUE?

ABOUT SITUATION ....
....
ABOUT YOUSELF ....
....

WHAT HAPPENED?

....
....

HOW DID IT MAKE YOU FEEL?

....
....

HOW DID YOU REACT?

....
....

WHAT HELPS YOU SOOTHE YOUR ANXIETY?

....
....

Anxiety Journal

DATE   TIME

PLACE   SOURCE OF ANXIETY

PHYSICAL SENSATIONS

NEGATIVE BELIEVES

ABOUT SITUATION ....
....

ABOUT YOUSELF ....
....

WHAT FACTS DO YOU KNOW ARE TRUE?

ABOUT SITUATION ....
....

ABOUT YOUSELF ....
....

WHAT HAPPENED?

....
....

HOW DID IT MAKE YOU FEEL?

....
....

HOW DID YOU REACT?

....
....

WHAT HELPS YOU SOOTHE YOUR ANXIETY?

....
....

DATE _____ TIME _____
PLACE _____ SOURCE OF ANXIETY _____
PHYSICAL SENSATIONS _____

NEGATIVE BELIEVES

ABOUT SITUATION ....
....

ABOUT YOUSELF ....
....

WHAT FACTS DO YOU KNOW ARE TRUE?

ABOUT SITUATION ....
....

ABOUT YOUSELF ....
....

WHAT HAPPENED?

....
....

HOW DID IT MAKE YOU FEEL?

....
....

HOW DID YOU REACT?

....
....

WHAT HELPS YOU SOOTHE YOUR ANXIETY?

....
....

Anxiety Journal

DATE   TIME

PLACE   SOURCE OF ANXIETY

PHYSICAL SENSATIONS

NEGATIVE BELIEVES

ABOUT SITUATION ....
....

ABOUT YOUSELF ....
....

WHAT FACTS DO YOU KNOW ARE TRUE?

ABOUT SITUATION ....
....

ABOUT YOUSELF ....
....

WHAT HAPPENED?

....
....

HOW DID IT MAKE YOU FEEL?

....
....

HOW DID YOU REACT?

....
....

WHAT HELPS YOU SOOTHE YOUR ANXIETY?

....
....

Anxiety Journal

DATE .... TIME ....

PLACE .... SOURCE OF ANXIETY ....

PHYSICAL SENSATIONS ....

NEGATIVE BELIEVES

ABOUT SITUATION ....
....

ABOUT YOUSELF ....
....

WHAT FACTS DO YOU KNOW ARE TRUE?

ABOUT SITUATION ....
....

ABOUT YOUSELF ....
....

WHAT HAPPENED?

....
....

HOW DID IT MAKE YOU FEEL?

....
....

HOW DID YOU REACT?

....
....

WHAT HELPS YOU SOOTHE YOUR ANXIETY?

....
....

DATE   TIME

PLACE   SOURCE OF ANXIETY

PHYSICAL SENSATIONS

NEGATIVE BELIEVES

ABOUT SITUATION ....
....

ABOUT YOUSELF ....
....

WHAT FACTS DO YOU KNOW ARE TRUE?

ABOUT SITUATION ....
....

ABOUT YOUSELF ....
....

WHAT HAPPENED?

....
....

HOW DID IT MAKE YOU FEEL?

....
....

HOW DID YOU REACT?

....
....

WHAT HELPS YOU SOOTHE YOUR ANXIETY?

....
....

Anxiety Journal

DATE .... **TIME** ....

PLACE .... **SOURCE OF ANXIETY** ....

PHYSICAL SENSATIONS ....

NEGATIVE BELIEVES

ABOUT SITUATION ....
....

ABOUT YOUSELF ....
....

WHAT FACTS DO YOU KNOW ARE TRUE?

ABOUT SITUATION ....
....

ABOUT YOUSELF ....
....

WHAT HAPPENED?

....
....

HOW DID IT MAKE YOU FEEL?

....
....

HOW DID YOU REACT?

....
....

WHAT HELPS YOU SOOTHE YOUR ANXIETY?

....
....

Anxiety Journal

DATE   TIME

PLACE   SOURCE OF ANXIETY

PHYSICAL SENSATIONS

NEGATIVE BELIEVES

ABOUT SITUATION ....
....

ABOUT YOUSELF ....
....

WHAT FACTS DO YOU KNOW ARE TRUE?

ABOUT SITUATION ....
....

ABOUT YOUSELF ....
....

WHAT HAPPENED?

....
....

HOW DID IT MAKE YOU FEEL?

....
....

HOW DID YOU REACT?

....
....

WHAT HELPS YOU SOOTHE YOUR ANXIETY?

....
....

Anxiety Journal

DATE .... TIME ....

PLACE .... SOURCE OF ANXIETY ....

PHYSICAL SENSATIONS ....

NEGATIVE BELIEVES

ABOUT SITUATION ....
....

ABOUT YOUSELF ....
....

WHAT FACTS DO YOU KNOW ARE TRUE?

ABOUT SITUATION ....
....

ABOUT YOUSELF ....
....

WHAT HAPPENED?

....
....

HOW DID IT MAKE YOU FEEL?

....
....

HOW DID YOU REACT?

....
....

WHAT HELPS YOU SOOTHE YOUR ANXIETY?

....
....

Anxiety Journal

DATE TIME

PLACE SOURCE OF ANXIETY

PHYSICAL SENSATIONS

NEGATIVE BELIEVES

ABOUT SITUATION ....
....

ABOUT YOUSELF ....
....

WHAT FACTS DO YOU KNOW ARE TRUE?

ABOUT SITUATION ....
....

ABOUT YOUSELF ....
....

WHAT HAPPENED?

....
....

HOW DID IT MAKE YOU FEEL?

....
....

HOW DID YOU REACT?

....
....

WHAT HELPS YOU SOOTHE YOUR ANXIETY?

....
....

Anxiety Journal

DATE .... **TIME** ....

PLACE .... **SOURCE OF ANXIETY** ....

PHYSICAL SENSATIONS ....

NEGATIVE BELIEVES

ABOUT SITUATION ....
....

ABOUT YOUSELF ....
....

WHAT FACTS DO YOU KNOW ARE TRUE?

ABOUT SITUATION ....
....

ABOUT YOUSELF ....
....

WHAT HAPPENED?

....
....

HOW DID IT MAKE YOU FEEL?

....
....

HOW DID YOU REACT?

....
....

WHAT HELPS YOU SOOTHE YOUR ANXIETY?

....
....

Anxiety Journal

DATE   TIME

PLACE   SOURCE OF ANXIETY

PHYSICAL SENSATIONS

NEGATIVE BELIEVES

ABOUT SITUATION ....
....

ABOUT YOUSELF ....
....

WHAT FACTS DO YOU KNOW ARE TRUE?

ABOUT SITUATION ....
....

ABOUT YOUSELF ....
....

WHAT HAPPENED?

....
....

HOW DID IT MAKE YOU FEEL?

....
....

HOW DID YOU REACT?

....
....

WHAT HELPS YOU SOOTHE YOUR ANXIETY?

....
....

Anxiety Journal

DATE .... **TIME** ....

PLACE .... **SOURCE OF ANXIETY** ....

PHYSICAL SENSATIONS ....

NEGATIVE BELIEVES

ABOUT SITUATION ....
....

ABOUT YOUSELF ....
....

WHAT FACTS DO YOU KNOW ARE TRUE?

ABOUT SITUATION ....
....

ABOUT YOUSELF ....
....

WHAT HAPPENED?

....
....

HOW DID IT MAKE YOU FEEL?

....
....

HOW DID YOU REACT?

....
....

WHAT HELPS YOU SOOTHE YOUR ANXIETY?

....
....

Anxiety Journal

DATE TIME

PLACE SOURCE OF ANXIETY

PHYSICAL SENSATIONS

NEGATIVE BELIEVES

ABOUT SITUATION ....
....

ABOUT YOUSELF ....
....

WHAT FACTS DO YOU KNOW ARE TRUE?

ABOUT SITUATION ....
....

ABOUT YOUSELF ....
....

WHAT HAPPENED?

....
....

HOW DID IT MAKE YOU FEEL?

....
....

HOW DID YOU REACT?

....
....

WHAT HELPS YOU SOOTHE YOUR ANXIETY?

....
....

Anxiety Journal

DATE .... **TIME** ....

PLACE .... **SOURCE OF ANXIETY** ....

PHYSICAL SENSATIONS ....

NEGATIVE BELIEVES

ABOUT SITUATION ....
....

ABOUT YOUSELF ....
....

WHAT FACTS DO YOU KNOW ARE TRUE?

ABOUT SITUATION ....
....

ABOUT YOUSELF ....
....

WHAT HAPPENED?

....
....

HOW DID IT MAKE YOU FEEL?

....
....

HOW DID YOU REACT?

....
....

WHAT HELPS YOU SOOTHE YOUR ANXIETY?

....
....

Anxiety Journal

DATE   TIME

PLACE   SOURCE OF ANXIETY

PHYSICAL SENSATIONS

NEGATIVE BELIEVES

ABOUT SITUATION ....
....

ABOUT YOUSELF ....
....

WHAT FACTS DO YOU KNOW ARE TRUE?

ABOUT SITUATION ....
....

ABOUT YOUSELF ....
....

WHAT HAPPENED?

....
....

HOW DID IT MAKE YOU FEEL?

....
....

HOW DID YOU REACT?

....
....

WHAT HELPS YOU SOOTHE YOUR ANXIETY?

....
....

Anxiety Journal

DATE .... **TIME** ....

PLACE .... **SOURCE OF ANXIETY** ....

PHYSICAL SENSATIONS ....

NEGATIVE BELIEVES

ABOUT SITUATION ....
....

ABOUT YOUSELF ....
....

WHAT FACTS DO YOU KNOW ARE TRUE?

ABOUT SITUATION ....
....

ABOUT YOUSELF ....
....

WHAT HAPPENED?

....
....

HOW DID IT MAKE YOU FEEL?

....
....

HOW DID YOU REACT?

....
....

WHAT HELPS YOU SOOTHE YOUR ANXIETY?

....
....

Anxiety Journal

DATE   TIME

PLACE   SOURCE OF ANXIETY

PHYSICAL SENSATIONS

NEGATIVE BELIEVES

ABOUT SITUATION ....
....

ABOUT YOUSELF ....
....

WHAT FACTS DO YOU KNOW ARE TRUE?

ABOUT SITUATION ....
....

ABOUT YOUSELF ....
....

WHAT HAPPENED?

....
....

HOW DID IT MAKE YOU FEEL?

....
....

HOW DID YOU REACT?

....
....

WHAT HELPS YOU SOOTHE YOUR ANXIETY?

....
....

Anxiety Journal

DATE _____ **TIME** _____

PLACE _____ **SOURCE OF ANXIETY** _____

PHYSICAL SENSATIONS _____

NEGATIVE BELIEVES

ABOUT SITUATION ....
....

ABOUT YOUSELF ....
....

WHAT FACTS DO YOU KNOW ARE TRUE?

ABOUT SITUATION ....
....

ABOUT YOUSELF ....
....

WHAT HAPPENED?

....
....

HOW DID IT MAKE YOU FEEL?

....
....

HOW DID YOU REACT?

....
....

WHAT HELPS YOU SOOTHE YOUR ANXIETY?

....
....

Anxiety Journal

DATE　　　　　　　　　　　　　TIME

PLACE　　　　　　　　　　　　SOURCE OF ANXIETY

PHYSICAL SENSATIONS

NEGATIVE BELIEVES

ABOUT SITUATION ....
....

ABOUT YOUSELF ....
....

WHAT FACTS DO YOU KNOW ARE TRUE?

ABOUT SITUATION ....
....

ABOUT YOUSELF ....
....

WHAT HAPPENED?

....
....

HOW DID IT MAKE YOU FEEL?

....
....

HOW DID YOU REACT?

....
....

WHAT HELPS YOU SOOTHE YOUR ANXIETY?

....
....